KU-066-297

Council

CANADA WATER LIBRARY
21 Surrey Quays Road
London SE16 7AR

10/22

www.southwark.gov.uk/libraries  @SouthwarkLibs

Please return/renew this item by
the last date shown.
Books may also be renewed by
phone and Internet.

OXFORD
UNIVERSITY PRESS

Great Clarendon Street, Oxford OX2 6DP

Oxford is a registered trade mark of
Oxford University Press in the UK and in certain other countries

© Oxford University Press 2022
Text written by Clive Gifford
Illustrated by Ekaterina Gorelova and Ana Seixas

Designed and edited by Raspberry Books Ltd

The moral rights of the author and artist have been asserted
Database right Oxford University Press (maker)

First published 2022

British Library Cataloguing in Publication Data:

ISBN 978-0-19-278030-0

1 3 5 7 9 10 8 6 4 2

Printed in China

Paper used in the production of this book is a natural,
recyclable product made from wood grown in sustainable forests.
The manufacturing process conforms to the environmental regulations
of the country of origin.

Acknowledgements

The publisher and authors would like to thank the following for permission to use photographs and other copyright material:

Cover artwork: Ekaterina Gorelova and Ana Seixas; Photos: Pavlo S/Shutterstock; Aleksandr Bryliaev/Shutterstock and author. **Inside artwork:** Photos: p1(tl): Pavlo S/Shutterstock; p6: World History Archive/Alamy Stock Photo; p8: leonello calvetti/Shutterstock; p18: Pictorial Press Ltd/Alamy Stock Photo; p25: Potapov Alexander/Shutterstock; p28: Creative Stall/Shutterstock; p30-31: Frankvr/Shutterstock; p32: NisanatStudio/Shutterstock; p33: Mark Rademaker/Shutterstock; p34(l): Miceking/Shutterstock; p34(r): Anastasiia Novikova/Shutterstock; p35(l): Forgem/Shutterstock; p35(r): Agnieszka Karpinska/Shutterstock;

p39, p76: Alexey Seafarer/Shutterstock; p46: Harvepino/Shutterstock; p47: apple2499/Shutterstock; p61: StockBURIN/Shutterstock; p63: Panther Media GmbH/Alamy Stock Photo; p71: Walter Oleksy/Alamy Stock Photo; p79: Pyty/Shutterstock; p81: Michele D'Ottavio/Alamy Stock Photo; p84: dpa picture alliance/Alamy Stock Photo; p85: Paul Treadway/Alamy Stock Photo.

Artwork by **Ekaterina Gorelova**, **Ana Seixas**, Aaron Cushley, and Raspberry Books.

Every effort has been made to contact copyright holders of material reproduced in this book. Any omissions will be rectified in subsequent printings if notice is given to the publisher.

Contents

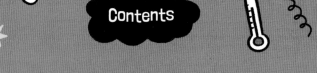

Chapter 1

What is Climate?

Climate is different from weather, which can change quickly from day to day (or even hour to hour). Climate is the typical weather, winds, rainfall, and temperatures found in an area over tens or hundreds of years.

Different regions of the world possess different climates. Regions with polar climates have long, cold winters and brief, cool summers whilst areas with a tropical climate are warm or hot all year round and receive a lot of rainfall. Scientists study and measure these climates and other factors, like the state of Earth's land and oceans, to get a picture of the planet's overall climate.

Earth is around 4.54 billion years old—

imagine the candles on that birthday cake. During its long lifetime, our planet's overall climate has changed many times. At times in Earth's history, it was so cold that ice covered North Africa where the Sahara Desert lies today.

Time for a dip!

Around 55 million years ago, it was so warm that instead of ice in the Arctic Circle, there were palm trees and crocodiles.

As you read this, Earth is in the middle of another change of climate, but what is causing so much worry is how fast it's changing. In the past, changes in climate have taken place naturally over thousands, sometimes millions, of years, but the latest change in global climate has taken less than 200 years to really get going. And, what's more, it's all our fault!

For thousands of years, people lived without affecting the planet's overall climate.

Then, from the 1750s, the Industrial Revolution changed things.

✹ Speak like a scientist ✹

THE INDUSTRIAL REVOLUTION

This period of great change began in Britain a little over 250 years ago and spread around the world. Beforehand, most people farmed for a living and objects were made by hand, one at a time. The invention of large machines, powered by steam engines, mass-produced a far greater number of goods than ever before, mostly in giant factories, which used up large amounts of energy and raw materials. Hundreds of thousands of people moved from the countryside to live and work in booming industrial towns and cities.

In **1750**, about **15%** of people in England **lived in towns**. By 1900, it was **85%**.

Large numbers of factories, metal–making industries, and railways sprang up. All of these burned vast quantities of coal (and sometimes wood) to produce heat or to provide power via steam engines. Later industries and machines, like motor vehicles, burned huge amounts of oil and natural gas as fuel.

All this burning sent gases up into the air.

At the same time, the human population started growing fast and many forests were cleared to create more farmland to grow food to feed them. As well as food, these extra people required clothing and other goods, leading to more industry and factories. This all meant more burning and **emissions**—the word used to describe substances that are released into the air.

All this activity has resulted in the entire planet's climate changing quickly. The average global temperature in 2020 was over 1.1°C warmer than 150 years before. That may not sound like much, but it's enough to **create BIG impacts.**

THE CAUSES AND IMPACT OF CLIMATE CHANGE

More droughts and floods are happening, devastating crops and communities.

Ice is melting.

There are more extreme weather events like hurricanes.

A warmer climate means more severe and longer-lasting wildfires.

Sea levels have risen 21–24 cm since 1870. They are predicted to rise far more in the years ahead.

The changing climate is altering animals' habitats, making it difficult for many to survive.

It may all sound pretty grim, but there is still hope. People have solved many problems in the past—from combatting diseases to thinking up new ways to obtain energy. Ingenious inventions and schemes already exist to help reduce the damage we're doing to the planet.

We just need to work together, really hard . . . and quickly!

This is a very short introduction to climate change, how it is caused, and what can be done to tackle it. Inside, you'll discover . . .

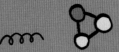

which **gases** cause most of the bother

why your **carbon footprint** weighs as much as an elephant

who planted one **million trees** before they reached their teens

how scientists time travel back over **100,000 years** to study the atmosphere

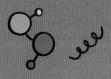

how **two million** Moroccan mirrors generate **clean, green** electricity.

Read on to first discover the changes happening **up in the air** . . .

Chapter 2

What is Atmosphere?

An atmosphere is a layer of gases that surround a planet. On Earth we have just the right combination of gases, known as air, to sustain life.

What's in the air?

Air is a mixture of different gas **molecules**. It is 78% nitrogen, 21% oxygen, 0.93% argon, a varying amount of **water vapour**, and small quantities of gases like **carbon dioxide** and **methane**. Animals rely on oxygen in air to breathe and turn their food into energy. Plants rely on carbon dioxide to make their food from a process called **photosynthesis**.

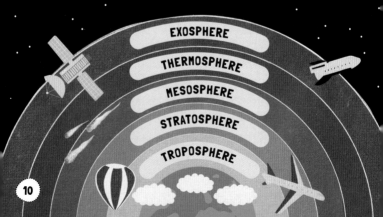

EXOSPHERE

THERMOSPHERE

MESOSPHERE

STRATOSPHERE

TROPOSPHERE

Earth's atmosphere is made up of **five different layers.** The troposphere is nearest and extends 7–15 km up from Earth's surface. Most of the clouds and weather are found in this layer. The farthest layer, the exosphere, extends hundreds of kilometres out into space.

Big benefits

Apart from providing living things with the gases they need, Earth's atmosphere performs other crucial tasks. For example, it **shields us from harmful ultraviolet (UV) radiation** from the Sun, because atmospheric gases, such as nitrogen and oxygen, absorb most of the Sun's UV rays. And the atmosphere burns up most of the millions of small pieces of whizzing rock and dust from space that head towards Earth, sometimes forming shooting stars.

 # Speak like a scientist

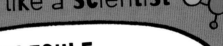

MOLECULE

A molecule is made from two or more **atoms** bonded together. It forms the smallest unit of a substance. For example, oxygen molecules in air are formed of two oxygen atoms, and a water molecule is made up of two hydrogen atoms and one oxygen atom.

Living in a greenhouse

Another benefit of our atmosphere is the **extra warmth** it provides us with. Like a cosy blanket, Earth's collection of gases do a good job of trapping some of the Sun's heat energy that strikes our planet. This is called the **greenhouse effect**, and without it our world would be a very different place. Scientists estimate that without this, the average temperature on Earth would be around −18°C—that's about 33°C lower than now. **Brrrr.**

Solar energy passes through the atmosphere.

ATMOSPHERE

Energy strikes and warms Earth.

A portion of the energy travels off into **space**.

Some energy reflects back as **infrared radiation** into the atmosphere.

EARTH

Atmosphere traps and re-emits some of the energy, warming the lower atmosphere and Earth's surface further.

Meet the greenhouse gases

The amount of **greenhouse gases** (GHGs) in the atmosphere is usually measured in parts per million (ppm) or parts per billion (ppb). **One ppb means there's one molecule of that gas in every one billion molecules of air.** Greenhouse gases are also measured by how long they stay in the atmosphere and how good they are at trapping heat.

Carbon dioxide (CO_2)

Amount: 416,000 ppb (all these figures are from January 2021)

People have sent more of this gas into the atmosphere than any other. Once it arrives, the **carbon cycle** (see pages 22–23) gradually removes some of the gas, but it's a slow process. Much of the carbon dioxide released today will still be present in the atmosphere centuries from now.

Methane (CH_4)

Amount: 1893 ppb

Methane doesn't hang around in the atmosphere too long— a maximum of twelve years. There's also far less of it than carbon dioxide, but it's still a powerful greenhouse gas. This is because it's able to trap thirty-five times more heat than carbon dioxide.

Nitrous oxide (N₂O)
Amount: 333 ppb

There's far less nitrous oxide in the atmosphere than the other major GHGs. Good job, too, as it can trap up to 300 times more heat than carbon dioxide and sticks around in the atmosphere for 110 years or so.

Fluorinated gases (F-gases)
Amount: less than 1 ppb

These human-made gases are used to make metals and electronic circuits. They are also found in some fridges and air conditioners. They can stay in the atmosphere for 10,000 years and some trap thousands of times more heat than carbon dioxide.

Water vapour (H₂O)
Amount: varies

Tiny droplets of water in the Earth's atmosphere are responsible for much of the greenhouse effect. They occur naturally as part of the water cycle—where water constantly travels between Earth's surface and the atmosphere, falling back to Earth as rain and snow. Warmer air holds more water vapour.

Hotting up

The amounts of greenhouse gases found in the atmosphere stayed at roughly similar levels for thousands of years. They only began rising sharply after the Industrial Revolution began.

Dr Charles Keeling was one of the first scientists to measure the amount of CO_2 in the air regularly. He began taking daily air samples in the Hawaiian Islands in 1958—they're still taken today. He plotted the amount of CO_2 in the air on a graph now known as the Keeling Curve. It provided persuasive evidence of a constant rise of CO_2 in the atmosphere.

ATMOSPHERIC CO_2 AT MAUNA LOA OBSERVATORY

Scripps Institution of Oceanography
NOAA Earth System Research Laboratory

PARTS PER MILLION

380
370
360
340
320

1960 1970 1980 1990 2000 2010 2020

CLIMATE CHAMPION

DR CHARLES KEELING

Produced the longest, uninterrupted evidence of CO_2's rise in the atmosphere.

Since 1750, CO_2 levels have increased by half—from 278 ppm to 417 ppm—higher than at any point in human history. There's also now a quarter more nitrous oxide in the atmosphere and more than two and a half times as much methane.

It turns out you *can* have too much of a good thing. The greenhouse effect, which has successfully warmed our planet to enable life, is now warming it more than before. All those extra greenhouse gases in the atmosphere mean less heat is heading out to space. Instead, **more is being trapped and reflected back to Earth.**

How do we know?

People weren't aware of the greenhouse effect in the past. The first inklings came when French mathematician Jean-Baptiste Fourier puzzled over Earth's temperature in the 1820s. He figured out that, given our distance from the Sun (about 149.6 million km), Earth should be a lot cooler than it was, meaning that something was helping to keep heat in.

In 1856, American scientist Eunice Foote found how CO_2 and water vapour both helped absorb more of the Sun's heat than regular air. Forty years after Foote, Swedish chemist Svante Arrhenius linked the amount of carbon dioxide in the atmosphere to the average temperature on Earth. More CO_2 meant higher temperatures.

Fourier, Arrhenius, Keeling, and Foote were some of the very first climate researchers. Since then, **thousands of scientists** have helped to **educate** us all **about Earth** and its **changing climate.**

At first my work was overlooked, and then male scientists got the credit. How unfair!

CLIMATE CHAMPION

EUNICE FOOTE

Discoverer of how substances absorb heat from the Sun.

Mounting evidence

For much of the 20th century, those who warned of dangerous changes in both the atmosphere and climate were doubted. But the evidence kept mounting up and up, and still does today. Thousands of samples of the atmosphere are now taken every year to measure the amounts of gases present. Detailed air, land, and sea temperatures are taken worldwide at scientific measuring stations and by space **satellites** orbiting Earth.

It is clear from all these measurements that the levels of greenhouse gases are rising and so is the average temperature of our planet. Each of the last four decades has been warmer than the previous one. In fact, nineteen of the twenty warmest years since accurate records began in the 1870s have all occurred between 1999 and 2020.

A people problem

In the 1990s, **ice cores** taken from Antarctica provided a record of CO_2 levels in the atmosphere stretching back 800,000 years. During all that time, they never passed 300 ppm. So, it's clear that something dramatic has happened in recent times for so much extra CO_2 (now at 417 ppm) to be present in the atmosphere.

✳ Speak like a scientist ✳

ICE CORES

These long thin cylinders are taken by drilling deep into very old ice, like coring an apple. The cores contain tiny bubbles of prehistoric air which can be analysed to get an idea of the atmosphere in the distant past.

The Intergovernmental Panel on Climate Change (**IPCC**) was formed in 1988 by the **United Nations**. Its experts examine thousands of pieces of climate research each year. Every four to seven years, it produces a reliable report. These reports are certain that people and their activities—like cutting down trees and burning oil and coal—are mostly to blame for the extra greenhouse gases in the atmosphere.

How much gas are we talking about? Well, a tonne (1,000 kg) sounds heavy. After all, it's about the weight of three grizzly bears or a class of thirty ten-year-olds.

Since 1850, scientists estimate that human activities have generated a staggering 2.2 million tonnes of carbon dioxide, much of which has reached the atmosphere. It's a mind-numbing amount.

According to the IPCC, carbon dioxide makes up three-quarters of the GHG emissions generated by people.

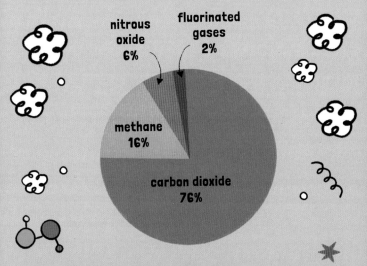

nitrous oxide
6%

fluorinated gases
2%

methane
16%

carbon dioxide
76%

So, where does all that carbon dioxide come from?

Let's find out.

Chapter 3

Where Carbon Comes From

There's a lot of carbon on Earth. Every plant, animal, and person contains carbon. An adult human weighing 70 kg contains around 16 kg of carbon atoms.

Carbon is constantly on the move, travelling through living things, the soil, water, and the atmosphere, mostly as carbon dioxide. This is known as the carbon cycle.

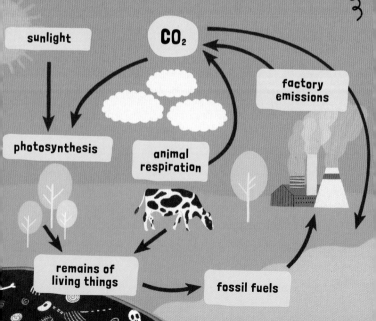

sunlight

CO_2

factory emissions

photosynthesis

animal respiration

remains of living things

fossil fuels

This is a simplified diagram of a complicated set of processes. The key ones to know about are:

1 Plants and animals already contain carbon. When they **respire** and make energy from their food, they produce and emit carbon dioxide. When a plant or animal is eaten by an animal their carbon travels further along the food chain.

2 Plants and algae absorb carbon dioxide from the atmosphere to make glucose food during photosynthesis.

3 When plants and animals die, their bodies are broken down by bacteria, fungi, and other living things, which all act as **decomposers**. The decomposers release carbon dioxide from the dead plants and animals into the air.

4 When decomposition doesn't happen completely, for example when there's not enough oxygen for everything to rot and break down, carbon may be stored in the ground. Over millions of years it can be squeezed, heated, and turned into **fossil fuels**, such as oil.

✳ Speak like a scientist ✳

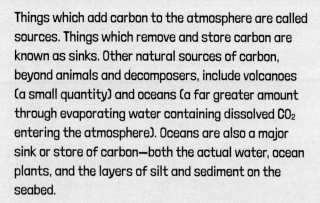

FOSSIL FUELS

Oil, coal, and natural gas were formed from the buried and fossilized remains of plants and animals that lived millions of years ago. They contain a lot of carbon and blaze fiercely, producing much heat when burned. Fossil fuels power the vast majority of motor vehicles and produce over 60% of the world's electricity.

Sources and sinks

Things which add carbon to the atmosphere are called sources. Things which remove and store carbon are known as sinks. Other natural sources of carbon, beyond animals and decomposers, include volcanoes (a small quantity) and oceans (a far greater amount through evaporating water containing dissolved CO_2 entering the atmosphere). Oceans are also a major sink or store of carbon—both the actual water, ocean plants, and the layers of silt and sediment on the seabed.

The other major natural **carbon sinks** are the world's forests. A 2021 scientific study showed that these absorbed a lot more carbon than they emitted—

around **7.6 billion tonnes of CO_2 every year between 2001 and 2019.**
That's almost 1,000 kg for every person on the planet.

For thousands of years, the mixture of sinks and sources kept the carbon cycle balanced. Human activities have upset this balance and the result is far more CO_2 in the atmosphere.

Cutting down trees

People have valued wood for thousands of years both as a fuel and a really versatile building material. It is only since the Industrial Revolution, though, that the rate of forest removal, called **deforestation**, has really speeded up. Sometimes, it is for the wood itself. More often, it is to turn forests into farmland for crops or grazing cattle.

According to the United Nations, 4.2 million km^2 of forests were lost between 1990 and 2020. That's an area seventeen times larger than the size of the UK.

Cutting down trees releases carbon into the atmosphere and reduces the amount of carbon the remaining forests can absorb. It also removes tree roots, which help bind the soil together and provide homes for many living things.

A question of energy

Deforestation causes large amounts of CO_2 emissions, but it is nowhere near the biggest source of extra greenhouse gases.

Global greenhouse gases created by **human activities**

Farming, forestry, deforestation
18.4%

Energy use in industry
24.2%

Energy use in buildings
17.5%

Add up all the percentages in the balloons. Almost three-quarters of all the greenhouse gases we send into the air are from energy use. This includes fuelling cars and planes, lighting streets and buildings, and producing heat to work metals in factories.

The demand for energy has soared since 1900. At that time, few people had cars or home electric lighting and there were no aircraft, TVs, smartphones, or computers. There are now almost five times as many people as then—many of whom fly in planes, travel in motor vehicles, and use dozens of electrical devices every day.

We rely on electricity partly because it is so versatile. It can easily be turned into many other forms of energy including heat, light, sound, and mechanical energy to move things. It can also be carried long distances along power lines to where it is needed.

Making chemicals and cement
5.2%

Other energy
15.3%

Energy for transport
16.2%

Waste
3.2%

Electricity itself causes very little pollution or greenhouse gas emissions. Some of the ways it is generated, though, most certainly do, particularly those which involve burning fossil fuels.

COAL
38%

NATURAL GAS
23%

HYDROELECTRICITY
16.2%

NUCLEAR
10.1%

WIND, SOLAR, AND BIOFUELS
9.3%

OIL
2.9%

Fossil fuels

As part of the carbon cycle, fossil fuels are packed full of carbon atoms. When they're burned they release large amounts of heat energy but also a lot of carbon dioxide. Just one litre of petrol, a fuel derived from oil, produces around 2.3 kg of carbon emissions when burned inside a car engine.

There are now one billion cars on the roads, plus buses, trucks, and motorcycles. The vast majority of these burn fossil fuels and make up over 70% of all greenhouse gas emissions created by transport.

Even more fossil fuels are burned in power stations. There, they heat water into expanding steam which drives a device called a **turbine** to generate electricity. Coal, oil, and natural gas are also burned in boilers and furnaces to warm buildings or to provide heat for use in industry. There's also the energy used to dig or drill to obtain the oil, coal, or natural gas in the first place. It all adds up. In 2020, burning fossil fuels created 34.1 billion tonnes of CO_2 emissions. **That's HUGE!**

✳ Speak like a scientist ✳

FLARING

This is the burning off of unwanted gases at oil wells, oil refineries, and chemical plants. Flaring, as well as leaks from oil wells and gas pipelines, produces many tonnes of GHG emissions each year.

Making materials

Our modern world—from skyscrapers to bridges and tunnels—is built using materials like concrete, cement, aluminium, and steel. All involve large amounts of greenhouse gases in their creation. When one tonne of steel is produced, so is around 1.9 tonnes of CO_2. Aluminium generates more than four times the emissions of steel. This is because aluminium is found in the Earth's crust, locked inside a rocky ore called bauxite. Vast amounts of electricity are needed to extract aluminium from the rock.

Cement binds bricks and other building materials together. Mixed with gravel, water, and sand, it produces **concrete**—the **world's most popular construction material.** It is so popular that in the time it takes you to read this sentence, over 19,000 bathtubs full of concrete are used on building sites worldwide. Making cement accounts for over 5% of all human GHG emissions.

✳ Speak like a scientist ✳

CARBON FOOTPRINT

This is a measure of the impact of a material or product. The footprint totals up all the GHG emissions produced by a product being made, shipped, sold, used, and disposed of. It can also be used to estimate all the emissions that a company, country, or individual person is responsible for.

CO$_2$E

Short for carbon dioxide equivalent, CO$_2$e describes the amount of CO$_2$ needed to equal the impact of all greenhouse gases in a carbon footprint.

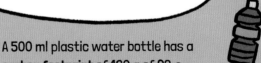

A 500 ml plastic water bottle has a **carbon footprint** of 160 g of CO$_2$e. That may not sound much but when you consider around **one million of these bottles are bought every minute, it quickly adds up.**

For a larger, more complex product, we need to add up all the emissions created in producing and delivering all its different raw materials, as well as the emissions created in making it. A new two-bedroomed house may have a carbon footprint of **around eighty tonnes.**

One clothing company estimated the **carbon footprint of a pair of its jeans** as **33.4 kg CO_2e.** This includes the emissions caused by growing the cotton to make the denim fabric, as well as the materials for the dyes, zips, and rivets, and the energy used in sewing and completing the jeans. It also includes the emissions created by washing the jeans during their lifetime. (Do you really need those new jeans?)

Services like transport can also have their footprints measured. Air travel, for example, generates a lot of emissions. A return flight from London, UK, to Rome, Italy has a footprint of 234 kg per passenger. London to New York, USA and back has a 986 kg carbon footprint for each person on board.

ETHIOPIA
0.17 tonnes

Personal footprints

INDIA
1.9 tonnes

A person can work out their carbon
footprint by totalling up all their individual
energy use in a year—from car journeys and
shopping to the electricity used by their
smartphones and computers. In the UK, the
average person has a footprint of around
5.4 tonnes CO_2e a year—about the weight
of an African elephant. People in other
nations have larger or smaller footprints.

BRAZIL
2.25 tonnes

FRANCE
4.8 tonnes

SOUTH KOREA
12.7 tonnes

**GLOBAL
AVERAGE**
4.93 tonnes

GERMANY
8.5 tonnes

US
15.5 tonnes

Footprints tend to be larger
the wealthier you are. A 2020
report by Oxfam showed that
the wealthiest 10% produced
over half of all human GHG
emissions. In comparison, the
poorest half of the planet
produced less than 10%.

KUWAIT
23.3 tonnes

Farm harm

A quarter of all human GHG emissions come from food—mostly from farming, but also transporting, selling, preparing, and disposing of food. **Cereal crops** like wheat, maize, and rice form almost half of all food eaten. An area almost the size of Peru is used just to grow wheat around the world. Certain crops, such as rice, produce a lot of methane as they grow.

Farms use over 200 million tonnes of artificial **fertilizers** every year to help boost the nutrients in the soil to make crops grow better. Making these fertilizers uses lots of energy and produces more GHGs than whole countries like France or the UK. Once applied, microbes in the soil convert some of the fertilizer into nitrous oxide, which also reaches the atmosphere.

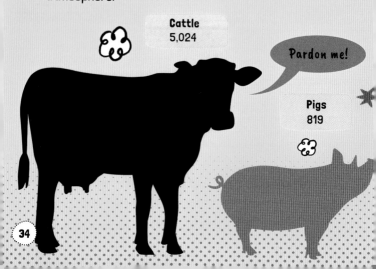

Cattle
5,024

Pardon me!

Pigs
819

More than four times as much land is used for rearing farm animals like cows and sheep than for growing crops. Large areas of forest and woodland have been cut down to create room for grazing livestock, which also consume huge amounts of fresh water. A third of all cereal crops grown are fed to farm animals as well, giving meat and dairy products a big carbon footprint.

Beef grief

Today, there are fractionally more cows than cars on the planet—around 1.4 billion. Each cow emits 250–500 litres of methane every day, mostly from burping! Their manure also releases GHGs, particularly methane. It all adds up and means that cows and cars have similar impacts on the atmosphere.

CO₂E PER TYPE OF ANIMAL
(in millions of tonnes)

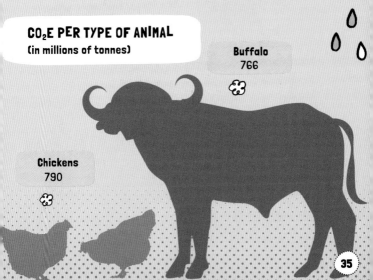

Buffalo
766

Chickens
790

What a waste

The next time you throw away perfectly good food, remember this statistic—around a third of all food is wasted. This totals 1.3 billion tonnes each year—about the weight of 10 million blue whales. A lot of land, effort, and around 3.3 billion tonnes of greenhouse gases were generated in order to produce that food.

× 10,000,000

WASTED FOOD per year weighs as much as 10 MILLION BLUE WHALES

Buried or burned

Food waste forms around 44% of all **municipal solid waste** (MSW). Food and other natural rubbish, such as paper and cardboard, release more greenhouse gases, especially methane, when they rot in giant rubbish dumps called **landfills**. Most rubbish either ends up here or is burned in plants called incinerators. These filter out some harmful gases created by burning, but many incinerators release some carbon dioxide and nitrous oxide into the atmosphere.

✸ Speak like a scientist ✸

MUNICIPAL SOLID WASTE (MSW)

This is the household rubbish collected from homes, schools, offices, and other buildings. The amount created varies from nation to nation. An average American produces over 800 kg of MSW a year, more than double the amount of a person in Japan and eight times more than a person in Bangladesh.

Yet more emissions are created by waste from industries and the thousands of rubbish trucks needed to carry waste away. A rubbish truck powered by fossil fuels creates more emissions than twelve entire homes!

If we don't tackle our mounting waste mountains, they could be producing emissions equal to 3 billion tonnes of CO_2 by 2050. That's a lot of rubbish, and just one of the ways the planet may feel different in the future.

Chapter 4

A Warming World

The world is already over 1.1°C warmer than it was when the Industrial Revolution began.

Scientists have produced lots of evidence of this warming. In 1998, Michael Mann and others plotted temperatures going back 1,000 years. The sharp rise in temperature in the past 120 years or so made the graph look like a tick or a hockey stick lying on its side.

Scientists have also proven that as greenhouse gases increase in the atmosphere, temperatures will continue to rise. Just how much is the BIG question.

In 2018, the IPCC produced a range of temperature estimates and a target. If everyone works really hard and makes major changes, it may be possible to limit the rise to 1.5°C higher than before massive industries were found around the globe. The IPCC dates this time as 1850 and calls it 'pre-industrial levels'.

If we do nothing, then temperatures could rise by 4°C or more by the end of this century. Such a rise would have **huge impacts on the planet.**

CLIMATE CHAMPION

MICHAEL MANN

US climate scientist whose 'hockey stick' graph prompted lots more debate and awareness of Earth's warming climate.

Northern Hemisphere.
Departures in temperature (C)
from the 1961 to 1991 average

YEAR BY YEAR DATA FROM TREE RINGS, CORALS, ICE CORES AND HISTORICAL RECORDS

YEAR BY YEAR DATA FROM THERMOMETERS

50-year average

Melting ice

Nearly all of the water on Earth—96.5% to be precise—is salt water, found in seas and oceans. Two-thirds of the world's fresh water is locked up as ice in **glaciers** and especially the large ice sheets close to the North and South Poles. As temperatures rise, more of this ice is melting and disappearing. As it goes, so do home territories for cold-loving creatures including walruses, arctic foxes, and polar bears.

Glaciers are rivers of ice found near the poles and on mountainsides. They are the source of many streams and rivers, but many are disappearing. In 1920, Glacier National Park in Montana, USA, was so named because it contained about 150 glaciers. By 2019, there were less than thirty. Around the world, most glaciers are retreating (getting smaller). Their melted ice flows along waterways and out into the oceans.

Arctic sea ice

The Arctic Ocean contains lots of sea ice (frozen sea water). The amount of ice increases and decreases with the seasons each year. Scientists measure the minimum level of sea ice each September, which is the end of the Arctic summer.

Since 1979, the Arctic sea ice minimum has dropped by over two-fifths. That's equal to losing an area of ice the size of Scotland each year. The depth of the ice is decreasing as well.

1980

2019

Shrinking
ARCTIC ICE

If temperatures continue to rise, there may be no summer ice in the Arctic at all in the future.

Speak like a scientist

ALBEDO

This is a measure of how well a surface reflects the Sun's energy. The whiter the surface, the higher the albedo and the more energy which bounces back. When sea ice melts, it reveals the darker ocean surface below which has a lower albedo, absorbs more energy, and reflects less. This warms the sea up, making it more likely that yet more sea ice will melt . . . and so on. Scientists call this circular set of events a feedback loop.

PERMAFROST

This is ground that is completely frozen and so microbes in the soil cannot decompose the plant matter found there. If ice disappears and the permafrost thaws, decomposing could release many tonnes of methane and other GHGs into the atmosphere.

Sea level rise

Rising temperatures also mean rising sea levels, for two reasons. Firstly, all the waters from shrinking glaciers, ice sheets, and disappearing sea ice adds lots of liquid to oceans. Secondly, most of the extra heat that reaches Earth's surface is absorbed by the oceans, and when water warms up, it expands. So, warmer water takes up more space, which helps push sea levels upwards. In the 2010s, the rise was about 3.6 mm a year.

No one knows how high the rise will be, but the IPCC predicts 0.29 m to 1.1 m by 2100. Such rises could submerge many marshes and other wetlands, and seawater could spoil some of our sources of drinking water. It may also mean more flooding.

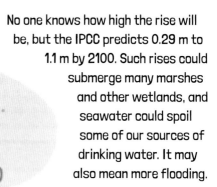

Some coastal towns and famous cities like Mumbai, New Orleans, and Shanghai will be under threat from rising seas and millions of homes along coasts and on islands might be ruined. In the case of particularly low-lying islands like the Comoros or the Maldives (which has an average height above sea level of only 1.5 m), it could mean the end of the islands themselves.

Changing chemistry

It's not only sea levels which are changing, so is the chemical make-up of ocean water. As the water gets warmer it is able to carry less oxygen, a vital gas for fish and other sea creatures. **Competition for the remaining oxygen may see some species dwindle in number or even die out.**

This is worrying for the millions of people who rely on fish and other seafood for much of the essential protein in their diet.

2100 sea level

2050 sea level

Oceans act as a major carbon sink (see page 24). They absorb more than a quarter of the carbon dioxide human activities have produced. Many scientists believe this has helped slow down the rate of climate change so far, but it has come at a cost. **The oceans are getting more acidic.**

More and more CO_2 enters the oceans from the atmosphere. There, it dissolves in the sea water and makes the water slightly more acidic. This **disrupts the delicate balance of ocean life in many ways**—scientists are still figuring them all out! The water weakens the shells and other hard body parts of some underwater creatures. It also appears to stop some species of fish from growing as well as they did before.

Speak like a scientist

CORAL BLEACHING

This happens when warmer water forces species of coral to eject the tiny colourful algae which live inside them, making the corals turn white. Some bleached corals die out. This is especially worrying because coral reefs provide homes for as many as a quarter of all ocean creatures.

Extreme weather events

The Earth's climate is complex, so predicting the weather is extremely difficult. But it's likely that many areas of the world will experience more examples of weather they're not used to. These might include sharp cold spells, massive snow blizzards or major **heatwaves**. These sudden and different conditions are called extreme weather events. Scientists believe they are becoming more common as the climate changes.

For every 1°C of extra warming, the atmosphere can hold 7% more water vapour, but this doesn't mean more rain for all. Changing rainfall patterns may see some places deprived of the usual amount of water they rely on. This may lead to water shortages, crop failures, and possible famines.

Other regions may start to receive far more rain than usual. Torrential rainfall may lead to **flash floods**, which can **wash away fertile soil, crops, roads, bridges,** and even **entire towns**.

Hurricanes, tropical cyclones, and typhoons are giant swirling circular storms, which have very powerful winds with speeds of up to 250 km per hour. They form out in the ocean, typically grow to 200–500 km wide (and some reach over 1,000 km wide), and can be deadly if they reach and sweep over land.

Climate change **may lead to even more** **powerful storms with faster winds and heavier rainfall.**

huge hurricane over Florida and Cuba

Fire!

Wildfires are a naturally occurring event in many regions of the world. But as the planet warms up and some regions become drier than before, more wildfires are occurring. In 2020, Australia suffered its largest ever wildfires. These blazed across 186,000 km² of land—an area bigger than England and Wales.

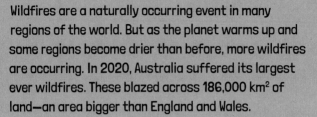

Fires in eastern Russian forests are shrinking the habitat of the endangered Siberian tiger, fewer than 550 of which are found in the wild.

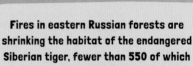

I'm running out of room to roam.

Wildfires can **spread rapidly and destroy large areas of forest, bush, and grassland,** all of which provide homes for other plants and creatures. If that wasn't bad enough, as the trees and plants burn, they send lots more carbon dioxide into the atmosphere.

Delicate balance

Wildfires and extreme weather, along with changing oceans and rainfall, can all disrupt the natural world. Many insects, reptiles, and amphibians such as frogs, for example, can only live within a narrow range of temperatures. If their home climate changes greatly, they may struggle to survive.

Many living things exist in a delicate balance with others in an **ecosystem**. They rely on each other in different ways. Scientists draw food chains and food webs to map out who eats what in an ecosystem.

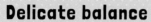

Speak like a scientist

ECOSYSTEM

This is a group of different living things, along with their surroundings. An ecosystem can be as small as a pond or rotting tree, or as large as a forest. It is made up of living and non-living things such as rocks, water, and soil.

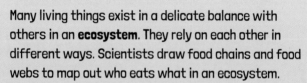

A **food web** shows all the feeding links between plants and animals in an ecosystem. It shows how food and energy passes along paths between living things.

I eat frogs, small mammals and rabbits.

I eat birds, small mammals and frogs. So watch out.

I eat slugs, snails and insects.

We eat insects. Delicious!

FOX

HAWK

FROG

VOLE

THRUSH

RABBIT

INSECT

SLUG

PLANTS

Even a small change to an ecosystem, such as less rain than before, can mean certain living things can no longer survive there. If they disappear, that may mean other living things cannot get the food they need. Scientists estimate that thousands of species of plants and animals are at risk of dying out as the conditions they live in start to change.

Invasion!

Climate change may, in future, drive more plants and animals away from their own ecosystems and force them to move or spread to new ones. The species that move could wreak havoc in their new homes, hunting home species or outcompeting them for food.

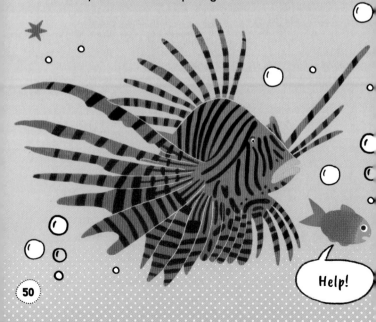

Help!

Lionfish have already spread from the Indian and Pacific Oceans into the Atlantic and even the Mediterranean Sea. Their stomachs can stretch up to 30 times their normal size when feeding. With no natural enemies in their new habitats, these greedy eaters can quickly outcompete other fish hunters like snappers and groupers.

Climate refugees

Climate change also affects people. In some places, people may no longer be able to grow the crops they did before or gather enough fish and seafood from the waters nearby. Coastal and island communities may have to move elsewhere as rising sea levels threaten their homes or jobs. This could lead to millions of climate **refugees** and conflict as people struggle over vital resources.

But don't despair. **There is hope. Honestly!**

There are **lots of things** that people can do as individuals, in groups, or as part of companies or whole countries, which scientists believe can stop many of the worst things from happening . . .

Chapter 5

Super Solutions

Good news! We've found out about climate change, what it is, and why it's happening. Now, we can look at ways in which to tackle it and slow it down.

Burning question

Burning fossil fuels creates an **enormous portion** of all the extra GHGs we're adding to the atmosphere. So, finding ways to supply everyone's energy needs in less harmful ways is the number one priority.

Wind power

Harnessing the wind to turn blades began with windmills, which were used to pump water and grind corn centuries ago. Modern wind turbines' blades are also spun by the wind, but the turbine drives a generator which produces electricity. Apart from the greenhouse gases that occur from building the turbine, they produce clean energy—energy that does not emit greenhouse gases or pollutants.

To generate a lot of energy, many wind turbines are grouped together in wind farms, on land or in the sea. Some turbines are enormous. The Vestas V164 is so named because each of its blades is 164 m long. Given enough wind, each machine can produce enough electricity for over 4,000 homes.

Wind turbines aren't perfect. They can be expensive to build and rely on a constant source of wind to work. Some people find they spoil the view and can be hazardous to birds. Despite these issues, wind power is booming. There are seventy times as many wind turbines generating electricity today as there were twenty years ago. In Denmark, they produce over 45% of all the country's electricity.

turbine blade

generator

gearbox

tower

grid connection

Solar power

As long as the Sun continues to shine (and it's good for a few billion years yet), its energy can be gathered and used for heat or to generate electricity. Solar thermal panels contain long, snaking pipes full of liquid which absorb the Sun's heat. The warmed liquid can then be used for heating or to provide hot water.

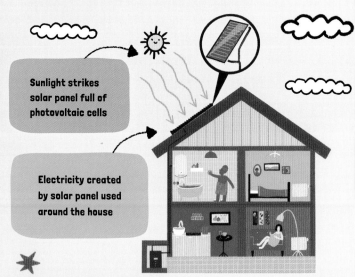

Sunlight strikes solar panel full of photovoltaic cells

Electricity created by solar panel used around the house

Photovoltaic (PV) cells are ingenious devices which convert sunlight into electricity. Tiny, individual cells may power a watch or pocket calculator but to produce greater amounts of power, the cells are packed together in large panels.

Solar panels cannot work in the dark but they do work on cloudy days, just not quite so well as on sunny ones, and new designs are getting more efficient. The panels are expensive, but they're becoming cheaper. In 2021, almost one-tenth of Australia's electricity was solar-powered, with a quarter of all houses in the country having solar panels fitted to their roofs. Photovoltaics also enable electricity to be generated in small, isolated communities a long way away from major power supplies.

An incredible 1.4 million panels are found at Europe's biggest solar power plant—Núñez de Balboa in Spain. It produces enough electricity to power 250,000 homes. A fossil fuel-burning plant of a similar capacity would emit around 215,000 tonnes of CO_2 into the atmosphere each year.

✳ Speak like a scientist ✳

RENEWABLES

Renewable energies like solar, wind, and wave power are replenished naturally and can be used for ever. In contrast, fossil fuels like coal and oil are non-renewable—their supplies will run out in the years ahead.

Hydroelectricity

Fast-moving water in rivers and large streams contains a lot of energy. In the past, this was converted into mechanical energy using waterwheels turned by the flowing water. Today, **hydroelectric** power (HEP) generates around one-sixth of the world's electricity without greenhouse gas emissions.

Although they can be incredibly costly to build, HEP systems are currently the most common renewable energy in use. The giant Itaipu HEP system built across South America's Paraná River supplies 90% of Paraguay's electricity as well as around 15% of Brazil's electricity needs.

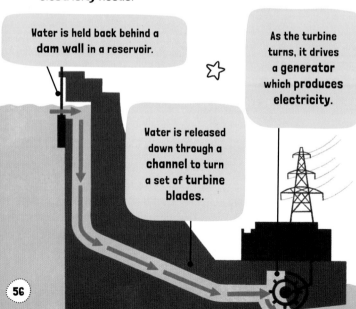

Water is held back behind a dam wall in a reservoir.

Water is released down through a **channel** to turn a set of **turbine blades.**

As the turbine turns, it drives a **generator** which produces **electricity.**

HEP systems produce electricity without direct GHG emissions, but they can have other impacts on the environment. Placing dams across rivers disrupts the movement of fish and other river creatures. They may involve flooding large areas of land leading to loss of homes for many creatures and thousands of people.

Waves and tides

People are only beginning to find practical ways to harness a little of the incredibly large amounts of energy held in the ocean's waves and tides. Small wave and tidal energy schemes are being trialled around the world. Some use long floating barriers which move up and down as waves pass or tides move in and out. The movement of the barriers is converted into electrical energy.

Nuclear power

Around 30 countries, including France, the UK, and the USA, generate some of their electricity by nuclear fission—splitting atoms. **Nuclear power** isn't renewable because it uses uranium for fuel which must be mined and processed, producing some GHGs. When up and running, though, nuclear power produces few emissions and can generate electricity more reliably than wind and solar power, whatever the weather.

Nuclear power produces radioactive waste which is harmful to living things. It makes dismantling old power stations extremely expensive. After accidents and leaks at several nuclear power stations including Fukushima, Japan, in 2011, many people are worried about further disasters.

✳ Speak like a scientist ✳

NUCLEAR FISSION

The nucleus (middle part) of an atom contains particles called neutrons and protons. Fission occurs when neutrons are fired at the nuclei of uranium atoms, splitting them up. The split nuclei release energy and some of their neutrons, which collide with other uranium atoms. Their nuclei split too, causing a chain reaction and lots of energy.

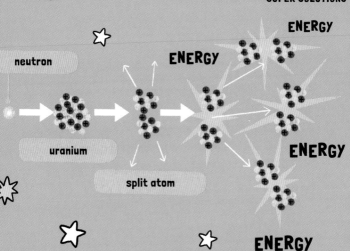

neutron

uranium

split atom

ENERGY

ENERGY

ENERGY

ENERGY

Underground energy

Geothermal power plants tap into the heat energy found underground in places where hot rocks lie below the surface. Cold water is pumped down long pipes into the hot rocks where it heats up. The returning hot water can provide heating or be turned into steam to power electricity generators.

Geothermal energy produces far fewer emissions than fossil fuel power stations and is popular in Kenya, the Philippines, New Zealand, and Iceland, where it creates over a quarter of the country's electricity, but geothermal plants can only be sited in places with suitably hot rocks within a few kilometres of the surface.

Using less energy

Another way of tackling the energy problem is to simply use less (energy conservation) or do more with the same amount (energy efficiency). For example, a person can conserve energy by walking rather than driving, or switching lights off when they no longer need them.

Why do I have to buy so much petrol?

If that person must drive, they can improve their vehicle's energy efficiency by removing any unnecessary weight, not using in-car air conditioning, and making sure the tyres are inflated correctly—to help the car travel further on the same amount of fuel.

More energy-efficient buildings are being designed to make use of natural light, warmth, and ventilation, so less energy is used for heating, cooling, and lighting. Manufacturers have developed more energy-efficient fridges and other appliances. In the United States, particularly energy-efficient lights and electrical appliances get an Energy Star label. These devices use much less energy than earlier models. The GHGs they saved in 2018 alone was equal to taking over seventy-one million cars off the roads.

Bright idea

One of the biggest energy efficiency improvements has come in electric lighting. Old **incandescent light bulbs** heat a piece of wire called a filament until it glows and produces light. Only 10% of the electricity used becomes light; the rest is wasted as heat. Modern Compact Fluorescent Lamps (CFLs) and Light Emitting Diode (LED) lights not only last longer than incandescent lights, but convert up to 85–90% of electricity into light, so they use much less energy.

INCANDESCENT BULBS—not such a bright idea

Reforestation

Replacing many of the trees lost to deforestation will aid the planet in a number of ways. It will help prevent some flooding, improve soils, and provide habitats for more living things. All the new trees mean that forests can store much more carbon, so that less heads off into the atmosphere.

According to the Woodland Trust in the UK, one hectare of different kinds of young trees can store as much as 400 tonnes of carbon.

Tree-planting schemes range in size. Some start small and local, and grow in scale. Felix Finkbeiner was just nine years old when he started a campaign to plant more trees in Germany. Within three years, his Plant-for-the-Planet scheme had planted one million trees. Brilliant!

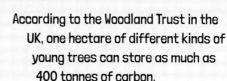

In 2019, Ethiopia managed to plant millions of trees in a single day, and the country plans to plant billions more. Costa Rica has already planted so many extra trees that it has more than doubled its forest cover from 1980s levels.

CLIMATE CHAMPION

FELIX FINKBEINER

German environmentalist who founded Plant-for-the-Planet as a schoolboy.

Carbon storage

Technology can help provide another type of carbon sink in the form of carbon collection and storage (CCS) systems. Carbon dioxide is collected at factories and power stations before it reaches the atmosphere. The CO_2 is then cooled to turn it into a liquid and pumped deep underground into spaces such as empty coal mines and oil wells. Already, several dozen CCS systems are working but many more will be needed to make a major difference.

Cleaner transport

Vehicles that burn fossil fuels emit around 10% of all GHG emissions. There are many ways this can be reduced. Some cities promote car sharing so that each vehicle carries extra passengers. Others, like Oslo in Norway, have banned private cars from large areas of their city centres.

Fully electric vehicles (EVs) produce no emissions as they run, although the electricity that powers them may have created GHGs. These emissions, though, typically add up to far less than a similar-sized petrol-fuelled car.

Transport CO$_2$

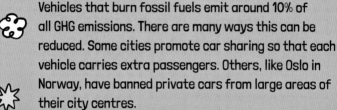

SHORT FLIGHT:
255 g CO$_2$ per km

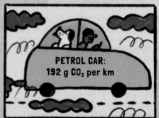

PETROL CAR:
192 g CO$_2$ per km

PETROL BUS:
105 g CO$_2$ per km

ELECTRIC CAR:
53 g CO$_2$ per km

Public transport is generally more energy efficient than private cars as buses, trains, trams, etc, carry more passengers for each unit of energy used. Large, long-distance electric trains like the TGV in France may produce as little as 3.2 g of emissions for every passenger kilometre. It means that taking a 500 km trip by train produces a carbon footprint of 1.6 kg compared to 96 kg in a car!

Material matters

We live in a wasteful world where new materials are produced, used and thrown away without a second thought. Cutting back on the materials we use and the amount we waste can save a lot of energy and emissions. The waste hierarchy on the next page shows the best order of actions to deal with materials and waste.

REDUCE

REUSE

RECYCLE

RECOVERY

DISPOSAL

Reducing **consumption** is best. It means buying less in the first place and avoiding unnecessary packaging.

Reusing and repairing products and materials helps reduce demand for new materials and the emissions they cause. For example, replacing single-use **disposable** plastic bags, cups and bottles with reusable items helps keep more materials out of landfills for longer.

Less desirable but still better than heading to the dump is using waste to produce energy by, for example, burning it to produce heat.

Recycling

It takes a lot of energy to produce new materials like steel and aluminium. **Recycling** materials requires far less energy and thus saves emissions. Recycling aluminium uses 90–95% less energy than producing

new aluminium from scratch. As a result, recycling one tonne of aluminium drinks cans or car parts saves around nine tonnes of CO_2.

Climate adaptation

Adaptations involve adjusting ways of life and doing things differently to live in a changing world. For example, as the planet's temperature rises, some crops will no longer grow as well as they used to in some places, so people are experimenting with new, heat-resistant versions of crops. Some countries are encouraging farmers to grow entirely different crops to adapt to the changing climate.

CANS

An example of an adaption is to build sea walls and other defences to protect part of the coast from future sea level rises. Sea defences can be built of hard materials like concrete and steel, or soft materials, using the natural landscape to build earth dykes and ditches. In parts of Fiji, people are planting forests of mangrove trees along the coast. These trees, which can grow in salty water, help reduce the height of waves that strike the shore and trap sediments from the sea to form new soil.

✳ Speak like a scientist ✳

AGROFORESTRY

This adaptation is the growing of trees, shrubs and crops together in the same fields, so the different species improve the soil and benefit one another. For example, cacao, whose beans are used to make chocolate, can benefit from shade and nutrients provided by mangoes and cashew trees.

Many adaptations can be simple such as homes using containers to store rainwater to guard against droughts, and planting trees in towns to provide cooling shade for the streets below.

Some adaptations, though, cost much more. These include building major flood defences, moving entire communities to higher ground, or launching space satellites to forecast storms more accurately. Governments have to consider costs and impact when forming adaptation plans for the future.

Chapter 6

Making Changes

All around the world, change is happening for the good. Every week, thousands of new solar panels and hundreds of new wind turbines are installed. China produced 120 times more clean electricity from wind power in 2020 than it did fifteen years earlier.

Success stories

In 2020, India's Pavagada Solar Park began generating enough electricity for 700,000 homes. In Morocco, the Noor Ouarzazate complex is the largest concentrated solar farm in the world. It uses two million mirrors to focus the Sun's heat to provide emissions-free electricity for thousands of homes and factories.

Morocco is aiming for just over half of all its energy to be produced by renewables by 2030. Some countries fortunate to have the geography to harness lots of geothermal and hydroelectric power have even higher rates. In 2020, Costa Rica generated over 98% of its electricity using renewables.

Electric vehicles are becoming more common, reducing the use of petrol and **diesel**. In 2020, a quarter of all new cars bought in the Netherlands and three-quarters in Norway were electric vehicles. In Denmark, many cities now only buy emissions-free electric buses for their public transport systems.

Many people are following in the footsteps of Kenyan activist, Wangari Maathai, and planting more trees than before. Maathai's campaigning saw 20 million new trees in Kenya and millions more in other African nations, for which she won the Nobel Peace Prize.

CLIMATE CHAMPION

WANGARI MAATHAI

Founded the Green Belt movement and campaigned for women to plant millions of trees.

71

Other people and nations are starting to recycle far more of their waste. Germany leads the way with over 60% of waste recycled, whilst Taiwan and South Korea manage more than half. South Korea is also a world leader in recycling food waste, turning most into **compost** or animal feed. In 1995, just 2% of its food waste was recycled. Today, that figure is 95%.

These are just a handful of success stories already happening, but the planet needs far more of them . . . and fast! **So why isn't change occurring more quickly?** There are a number of reasons.

I don't believe it!

Scientists have been battling non–believers for decades. Some people simply do not accept that the climate is actually changing or that carbon dioxide can have such a big impact. Others accept that CO_2 is mounting, but refuse to believe it is people's fault. Science has proven these viewpoints wrong, but many still feel that the problem is exaggerated and might go away.

What's wrong with a few degrees warmer? I like the Sun.

I'm not giving up fast cars or hamburgers for anything!

I don't trust scientists. They can't even get tomorrow's weather right.

Climate change won't happen in my lifetime. I'm not changing.

I recycle, don't drive or eat meat. Why should I pay for it?

It's too complex and I'm far too busy. I'll leave it to others to sort out.

Vested interests

Attacks on climate science have often come from the companies and individuals who have grown wealthy by selling or using fossil fuels. They have been keen to keep things the way they are and are fearful that new laws and targets will affect their business. These 'vested interests' use the media to spread **untrue claims** and make people believe they might lose their jobs. They are one reason why many people were slow to accept the climate change emergency as **science fact.**

There's no problem with fossil fuels.

Now or never

Would you give up burgers, chocolate, screen time, or holidays abroad to help save the planet? Not everyone would. Tackling climate change may call for sacrifices now, with the benefits not seen for many years. The trouble is that people struggle to think very far ahead and prefer their rewards now or soon, rather than a long way into the future.

Politicians are often voted in for short periods of time and need to stay popular to be re-elected. So, many focus on **short-term things**. Some may avoid making tough **long-term decisions**, especially ones that involve upsetting their country's voters by asking them to make large sacrifices. This can sometimes result in problems being left for others to solve in the future.

A costly business

Some changes could cost countries billions, but scientists argue that **the cost of doing nothing is far greater.** The UK National Audit Office, for instance, estimates that for every one thousand pounds spent on protecting communities from flooding, nine thousand pounds of flood damage costs are avoided.

In agreement?

Another major obstacle to progress is getting all the 200 or so nations of the world to agree on precisely how climate change should be tackled. International agreements have been signed many times in the past but without much success.

> *I'll believe it when I see it.*

One part of the problem is that different countries feel differently about some of climate change's likely impacts. A low-lying nation such as Bangladesh, for example, may feel more strongly about flooding than a nation far from the sea. Similarly, a country that has grown rich producing and selling oil or coal may be more reluctant to phase fossil fuels out and lose jobs than one that has few cars and industries and relies far more on farming.

In 2015, there appeared to be some good news, when 196 countries committed to deliver the Paris Agreement. This far-reaching agreement promised to limit the average temperature rise to, 'well below 2°C' compared to before the Industrial Revolution. The ideal target in the agreement is 1.5°C.

The IPCC estimates that for the 1.5°C target to be met, emissions need to start dropping quickly and halve by 2030. To achieve this target, the world must change fast. Deforestation must be halted, we must waste far less, move away from petrol-burning vehicles, and switch much more to low-carbon renewable energies like wind and solar power. The remaining fossil fuels on the planet need to stay where they are—**in the ground!**

One thing that makes targets harder to achieve is population growth. Every year, the number of people on the planet rises by around 80 million—almost the population of Germany. All these extra people need energy and resources.

When born into high income nations like the USA, UK, or Japan, a person is more likely to produce high emissions. The richer a country becomes, the more emissions it tends to produce. The US has 4.2% of the world's population, for example, but produces 15% of all the world's emissions. **Shouldn't countries who produce the most GHGs be doing a lot more than others?**

Poorer, low-income nations often have less industry and fewer motor vehicles, and produce lower levels of GHGs. Some of these countries want time and opportunities to build up their own industries. For many years, other countries have enjoyed the benefits of fossil fuels and the wealth that those industries have brought. Shouldn't they get the same chance? After all, up to this point, they are the least to blame.

In 2018, Kenya and South Korea had similar-sized populations (about 52 million) but South Korea produced thirty-five times more emissions than Kenya.

Helping and sharing

The effects of climate change are not shared out evenly around the world. Many of the world's poorest countries feel its impacts more sharply than wealthier nations. They may lack the money to adapt, already suffer from floods and droughts, and are often very reliant on farming, which is expected to be one of the hardest-hit areas of work.

Many of these nations believe they deserve far greater help. This may include money from wealthier countries as well as access to technologies like renewable energies to help them adapt.

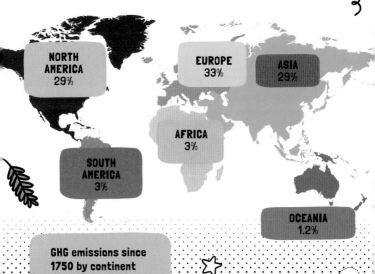

NORTH AMERICA
29%

EUROPE
33%

ASIA
29%

AFRICA
3%

SOUTH AMERICA
3%

OCEANIA
1.2%

GHG emissions since 1750 by continent

Planet protests

Concerned about the future, many have begun protesting both online and in public. In 2018, fifteen-year-old Swedish schoolgirl Greta Thunberg began school strikes to protest against climate change and her country's lack of progress. Her personal campaign gained many followers on social media and **sparked thousands of school strikes and demonstrations worldwide.** The millions of young people helped put climate change firmly in the news and raised further awareness of the problem.

I'M SKIPPING LESSONS TO TEACH YOU ONE

SKOLSTREJ
FÖR
KLIMATET

The protests also put pressure on politicians to take more urgent action and speed up change to meet the targets in the Paris Agreement.

CLIMATE CHAMPION

GRETA THUNBERG

Young activist who helped mobilize millions of young people to protest for action to tackle climate change.

The protests show how deeply young people care about tackling climate change and how they are prepared to **take action** to help the planet they will be inheriting.

STRIKE
TO SAVE
MY FUTURE

Chapter 7

How Can I Help?

Climate change can feel overwhelming. It can be tempting to think that the problem is just too big for you to take on. But remember, you are not alone. Neither do you have to do as much as Greta in order to make a real difference.

Think local, act global

As you read this, many kids, and adults, too, are busy cleaning up old canals or ponds, planting new trees, or running recycling schemes. Some help organize car-sharing, clothes swaps, or walks to school and after-school events to cut back on car journeys. Others arrange gatherings to learn more about climate change or to raise funds for environmental groups and causes.

Banding together with others can help you launch a local campaign, protest, or **petition** to get councils or companies to make positive changes. You can write to your local council or representative, such as a UK MP or US Congressman or woman. You can ask companies why they persist in an action that causes the planet harm. You can contact your local news media and community groups to publicize your campaign and produce fact sheets and posters to highlight the changes needed.

Some local actions snowball and **bring about big results.**

British sisters, **Ella** and **Caitlin McEwan**, started a petition in 2018 to get fast food chains to stop including disposable plastic toys with their children's meals. They felt that these toys had a large carbon footprint and were mostly thrown away, adding to the waste problem. Their petition gained over 500,000 signatures and led to many restaurants stopping the practice.

Ryan Hickman was only seven years old when he started Ryan's Recycling—collecting drinks cans and plastic and glass bottles for recycling. This young American has helped recycle over one million items so far. The money made has been donated to the Pacific Marine Mammal Center.

Melati and **Isabel Wijsen** were just ten and twelve years old in 2013 when they began a campaign to stop wasteful plastic bags and other items littering their island of Bali in Indonesia. The sisters organized beach clean-ups, gave talks, and arranged alternative bags to replace plastic ones. Their hard work resulted in a law banning single-use plastic bags and straws from the island.

84

William Kamkwamba was thirteen years old when he built a wind turbine out of junk to provide his home in Malawi with electricity for the first time. He built further machines to help his village including a radio transmitter and a solar-powered water pump. He has since founded the Moving Windmills Project to bring clean energy, technology, and education to remote areas of Malawi.

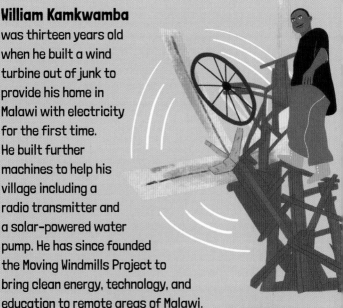

CLIMATE CHAMPION

WILLIAM KAMKWAMBA

Ingenious inventor of useful machines to aid poor, remote villages in Africa.

**LIGHTING AND
APPLIANCES**
14.1%

Saving energy

The more energy you and your household save,
the fewer greenhouse gases you're sending into the
atmosphere. Many actions like:

⚛ turning lights off
⚛ unplugging items when not in use
⚛ closing doors and windows when it's cold
⚛ opening them when it's warm

. . . are easy to perform and become energy-saving
habits. It takes a lot of energy to pump, treat, and
heat water, so the less you use, the more GHGs you
prevent. Take shorter showers, don't let the water run
whilst washing or brushing your teeth, and get adults
to fix any dripping taps. Use a bucket rather than a
hose to wash your muddy bike.

SPACE HEATING
63.6%

ENERGY CONSUMPTION
in a typical European Union
household is dominated by
heating and lighting.

Speak like a scientist

STANDBY POWER

This is electricity consumed by devices that are plugged in but not in use. A fully charged mobile, still plugged in, wastes 2–3 watts of electricity, whilst an idle desktop computer can use over 80 watts. These amounts, multiplied by many devices in a home and the long time they may be left plugged in, can really mount up. Unplug!

COOKING
6.1%

WATER HEATING
14.8%

In mild and cooler climates, home space heating makes up more than three-fifths of all home energy use. Reducing this even by a small fraction can make a sizeable difference. Getting your household to lower the central heating **thermostat** by 1°C can stop 360 kg of CO_2 emissions per year. **Imagine that repeated in every home!**

OTHER
1.0%

SPACE COOLING
0.4%

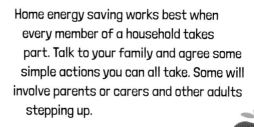

Home energy saving works best when every member of a household takes part. Talk to your family and agree some simple actions you can all take. Some will involve parents or carers and other adults stepping up.

Food for thought

Careful eating can help reduce your carbon footprint. This includes buying food with as little packaging as possible, such as loose fruit and vegetables. If there is packaging, make sure that it can be recycled by checking the labels. Another tip is to buy food that is grown and prepared locally. This can help cut back emissions involved in transporting food long distances.

Try to reduce food waste by making meals from leftovers, and if your home has a garden but no compost bin, campaign to get one. Turning waste food into natural compost for fertilizing the garden saves emissions created with waste and fertilizer—

a double win!

Wash cars and windows with a bucket of water not a hose.

Air dry your clothes rather than using an electric tumble dryer.

Cold day? Put an extra layer on instead of the heating.

Use energy-efficient CFL or LED bulbs.

Cut car trips by walking, cycling, or using public transport.

Warm day? Instead of switching on electric fans or air conditioning, open windows.

Ensure full loads in washing machines and dishwashers rather than more half-load washes.

Keep the fridge full and its door shut (as much as possible).

According to The Vegetarian Society, going **vegetarian** for a year **saves the same amount of GHGs** as **not driving** a family car for **six months.**

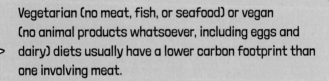

Vegging out

Vegetarian (no meat, fish, or seafood) or vegan (no animal products whatsoever, including eggs and dairy) diets usually have a lower carbon footprint than one involving meat.

If going completely veggie is not for you, then consider a Meat-Free Monday or eating less meat in general, especially beef (1 kg of beef has a carbon footprint of 36–60 kg). Hundreds of meat-free products and thousands of tasty recipes exist. If you can get friends or family to join you, then you multiply the effect at a stroke!

Climate-kind consumers

Remember the waste hierarchy on page 66? Try to follow it when buying and using items, starting with avoiding unnecessary purchases. **Ask yourself, do I really need this?** Can I use something I already have or borrow from someone else? If you must own something, try swapping with friends or buying second-hand, such as from charity shops.

Look to break the cycle of buying and throwing away regularly which creates high levels of waste and emissions. You can do this by repairing and reusing items as much as possible. Use both sides of pieces of paper and repair small tears in clothing rather than buying new items. Avoid disposable plastic bottles when you can simply refill and reuse the same bottle for long periods.

You now know what climate change is, its causes, effects, and some of the ways people can tackle it.

Hopefully, the end of this book is just the start of your journey ...

... **Maybe you feel motivated** to alter some of your habits, tackle local projects, or campaign for positive change. **Perhaps you feel inspired** to consider a career in climate or environmental science. Who knows, maybe people will be writing about you as a **CLIMATE CHAMPION** in the future.

Glossary

agroforestry the growing of crops, trees, and other plants together in the same fields

algae very simple small living things that mostly live in water

atmosphere the layer of gases which surround Earth or any other planet

atom a tiny object which makes up every kind of solid, liquid, and gas. It consists of a tiny, very dense nucleus surrounded by one or more electrons

billion one thousand million (1,000,000,000)

carbon cycle the circulation of carbon atoms between the atmosphere and Earth

carbon dioxide a chemical compound usually in the form of a gas. It is a greenhouse gas and also the gas people and animals breathe out

carbon footprint the amount of carbon emitted by an individual, company, or nation over a given period of time. Also, a measure of the amount of carbon emitted in the making and use of a product

carbon sinks ecological systems such as the oceans or forests which remove and store carbon dioxide from the atmosphere.

cereal crops species of grassy plants including wheat, whose grains are processed to produce food

climate the general weather conditions of a region over a long period of time

climate adaptation taking actions to deal with the effects of climate change already occurring or expected in the future

CO₂e short for carbon dioxide equivalent—the amount of CO_2 needed to equal the impact of all greenhouse gases in a carbon footprint

compost a mix of decaying plant matter, and sometimes manure, used to add nutrients to the soil

consumption the buying and using of goods and services

coral bleaching coral turning white after ejecting the colourful algae that live inside them, caused by warming seas

decomposer a living thing that breaks down dead plants and animals and releases the minerals they contain into the environment

deforestation the permanent removal of forests, an act that can lead to increasing carbon dioxide emissions

diesel a type of fuel derived from the fossil fuel, oil

disposable designed to be thrown away after use

drought a period of unusually dry weather resulting in serious water shortages and sometimes crop failures

ecosystem a collection of living and non-living things

emissions gases and particles released into the atmosphere, most commonly used to describe substances sent into the atmosphere by human activities

fertilizer a substance added to the land to improve the soil so that it can grow more crops

f-gases short for fluorinated gases, these are a group of powerful greenhouse gases that can stay in the atmosphere for hundreds or thousands of years

fossil fuels fuels such as coal, oil, and natural gas, which are formed over millions of years from the remains of living things, and produce lots of carbon dioxide when burned

geothermal energy energy obtained from heat found underground

glacier a large mass of ice created by compacted snow which moves slowly over land

greenhouse effect the insulating effect caused by some gases in the atmosphere which trap some of the Sun's heat and warm Earth's surface

greenhouse gases (GHGs) natural and human-made gases which cause the greenhouse effect, particularly water vapour, carbon dioxide, methane, and nitrous oxide

habitat the surroundings that a particular species needs to survive

heatwave an extended period of hotter than expected weather in a region

hydroelectricity electricity generated by moving water turning turbines

ice cores cylinders of ice taken by drilling deep into old ice

incandescent bulb a traditional style of lightbulb that heats a wire filament producing light but also wasting lots of heat energy

Industrial Revolution the change from goods being made in small quantities in shops or homes to goods being made in large quantities in factories

IPCC the Intergovernmental Panel on Climate Change, a body set up by the United Nations to review research on climate change

landfill the disposal of waste by burying it in the ground

methane a colourless, odourless greenhouse gas which occurs both in nature and as a result of human activities

molecule two or more atoms bonded together, which form the smallest unit of a substance

municipal solid waste (MSW) rubbish collected from homes, schools, offices, etc

nuclear power the splitting of the nucleus of atoms to produce energy used to generate electricity

permafrost ground that is completely frozen so that microbes in the soil cannot decompose its plant matter

petition a document signed by a lot of people asking a government, council, company, or another group to take a particular course of action

photosynthesis the process by which plants make food from water, carbon dioxide, and sunlight

photovoltaic cell a device that converts energy from sunlight into electricity

recycling the collection and processing of waste into new and useful materials and products

refugees people who have been forced to leave their home country due to war, persecution, or natural disasters

satellites machines launched to orbit the Earth and perform useful tasks such as photographing or measuring its surface

species a group of living things of the same kind

standby power electricity consumed by devices that are plugged in but not in use

thermostat a device used in heating systems that controls the temperature of a home

turbines a device with blades that can be turned by a force such as wind, water, or high pressure steam. Turbines are often used to drive generators which produce electricity

United Nations (UN) an international organization formed to promote international peace, security, and cooperation between countries

water vapour water in the form of a gas

Index